the
gram
is

the gram is

By Jerolyn Ann Nentl

Library of Congress Catalog Card Number: 76-24203. International Standard Book Number: 0-913940-47-X.

Design — Doris Woods and Randal M. Heise.

1 KILOGRAM **1 LITER**

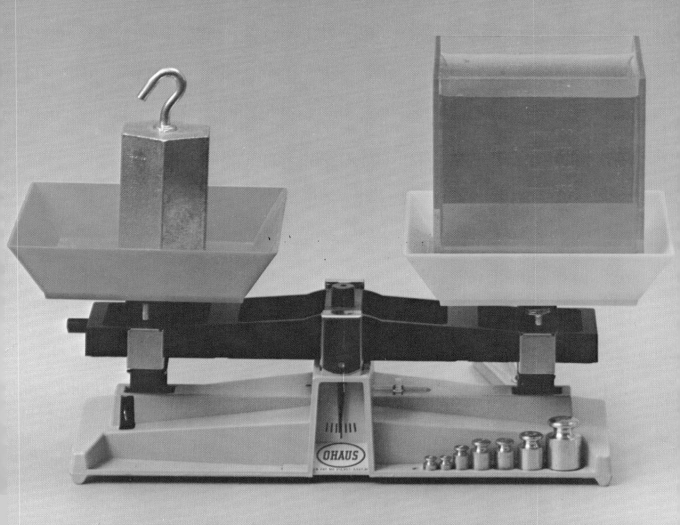

Special Thanks to:

Dr. Mary Kahrs - Professor of Education at Mankato
State University, Mankato, Minnesota

Mr. David L. Dye - Mathematics Consultant, St. Paul, Minnesota

PHOTO CREDITS

Mark Ahlstrom, Media House

R.M. Heise - Art Director

the
gram
is

When you are using the metric system and you want to know how much something weighs, you measure it in grams.

To give you an idea how much a gram is, hold two nickels in one of your hands. They weigh about 10 grams.

When you want to know how much something weighs you are really talking about "mass."

Mass means how much "stuff" there is in an object. It means how much matter there is in that object. In the example, the two nickels have a "mass" of 10 grams.

Weight really means something different. It is the force of gravity on a particular object.

The best example of what weight really means is the astronauts. The astronauts are the same people on earth as they are on the moon. They have the same bodies. They possess the same mass.

Since the moon is smaller and has less density, the force of gravity on the moon is only 1/6 of what it is on earth. So while they were on the moon, each of the astronauts weighed only 1/6 of what he did when he was on earth.

Do you remember how they bounced around when they walked on the moon's surface? That was because the gravity pulled less, and so they were much lighter in weight on the moon than here on earth.

In the United States people have used the word "weight" when they actually mean weight and also when they mean mass. So the real meaning has become confused.

You may begin to hear the word "mass" more and more often as people learn the real distinction between weight and mass.

From now on in this book, the word "mass" will be used. The two nickels you held in your hand have a mass of about 10 grams.

You combine those prefixes with the word gram just like you did with the words meter and liter.

DECIgram means 1/10 of a gram

CENTIgram means 1/100 of a gram

MILLIgram means 1/1000 of a gram

The prefixes for things with very little mass are the same as those you learned for the meter and the liter.

DECI means 1/10

CENTI means 1/100

MILLI means 1/1000

There is another way of saying this:

It takes 10 DECIGRAMS to make one gram.

It takes 100 CENTIGRAMS to make one gram.

It takes 1000 MILLIGRAMS to make one gram.

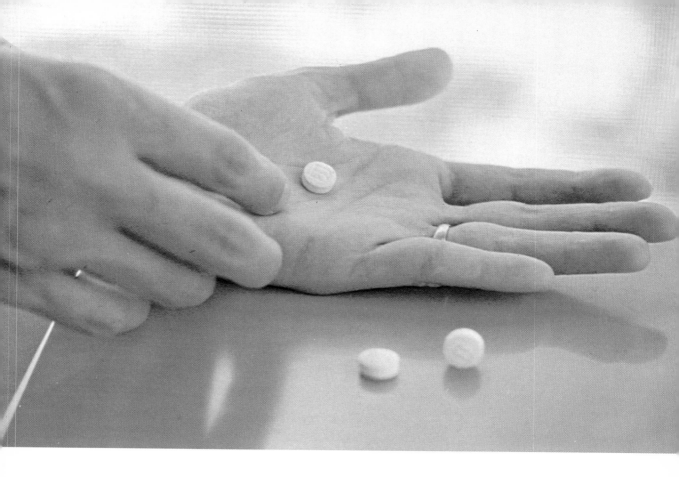

You will not see or use these units of measurement very often because they are so small. Ask an adult if you can hold three aspirin tablets in your hand to feel how little mass they have. Three aspirin tablets have a mass of about one gram.

You will not have to measure anything smaller than that very often, so you will not have to use decigrams, centigrams or milligrams very often.

Medicines and vitamins are examples of very small measurements of mass in everyday life. They are usually measured in milligrams.

To find the mass of bigger things the units DEKAGRAM, HECTOGRAM and KILOGRAM are used. The prefixes used with the word "gram" are the same ones you learned for the meter and the liter and they mean the same thing.

DEKA means 10

HECTO means 100

KILO means 1000

So it is easy to remember how many grams there are in a dekagram, a hectogram and a kilogram.

There are 10 grams in a DEKAGRAM.

There are 100 grams in a HECTOGRAM.

There are 1000 grams in a KILOGRAM.

There is one other unit of measurement for very large things. It is the metric ton and it is equal to 1 000 000 grams or 1000 kilograms. Sometimes you will see it written "tonne."

Of all these measurements that are bigger than a gram, it is the kilogram and the metric ton you will use most often.

This old 1927 caterpillar has a mass of about 13 metric tons.

Now you will see a very interesting thing about the metric system. The gram and the liter are related very closely.

Do you still have the liter box you made when you read the book, "THE LITER IS?" You can use it to see how the gram and the liter are related.

Be sure the liter box is lined with plastic. Then fill it to the top with water.

The amount of water that is in the liter box when it is filled to the top has the mass of about one kilogram.

The small box on the next page is 1 centimeter long, 1 centimeter wide, and 1 centimeter high. It holds 1 milliliter of water and weighs 1 gram. It takes 1000 milliliters to make 1 liter. It takes 1000 grams to make a kilogram.

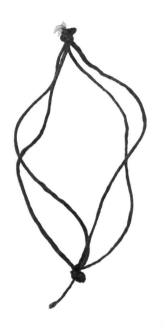

You can do some interesting experiments by making your own balance scale.

To make your balance scale, cut eight pieces of string or cord or yarn of equal length. Try making them about 50 centimeters long, using the meter stick you made when you read the book, "THE METER IS."

Now put four pieces in one pile and four in another pile. Then tie the four in one pile together in a knot at the top and in a knot at the bottom to make a sling.

Do the same with the other four pieces.

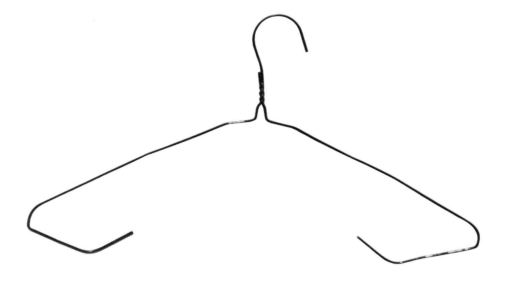

Next, take a coat hanger, and have an adult cut the middle part of the horizontal piece out, and throw it away. Turn up each end to make a hook. Also, turn the part you use to hang up the coat hanger sideways.

Now your coat hanger should be able to hang on a table edge. Does it? Be very careful of the sharp edges and use a piece of cardboard or other heavy paper to protect the table from scratches.

Hang one sling by one of the knots you tied on one hook and the other on the other hook. Next take two small saucers that have exactly the same mass and set one in each sling that you made. If you use plastic saucers you won't have to worry about breaking any dishes.

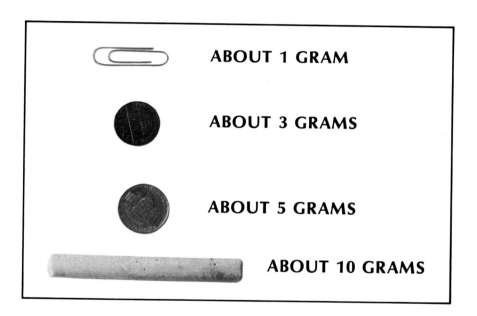

ABOUT 1 GRAM

ABOUT 3 GRAMS

ABOUT 5 GRAMS

ABOUT 10 GRAMS

To find the mass of an apple, put the apple in one saucer. Then put nickels, pennies, paper clips, or pieces of chalk in the other saucer until both saucers are straight across from each other, or balanced. Use the chart above to figure out how much the mass of the apple is. Now you are ready to begin other experiments.

You can try measuring the mass of:

a silver dollar

a ballpoint pen

or your favorite candy bar

a piece of fruit

a spool of thread

a baseball or a battery

Now try another way to find the mass of the same items, plus larger and heavier items. Use your liter box on one side of the balance scale, and an item on the other side. Fill the plastic lined box with just enough water to balance the scale.

To find out how much mass each thing has, just put each of the items on the saucer, and fill the liter box with water until both saucers are straight across from each other, or balanced. If the liter box cannot hold enough water to balance the scale, you know the item has a mass of more than one kilogram.

Your father probably has the mass of about 81 kilograms.

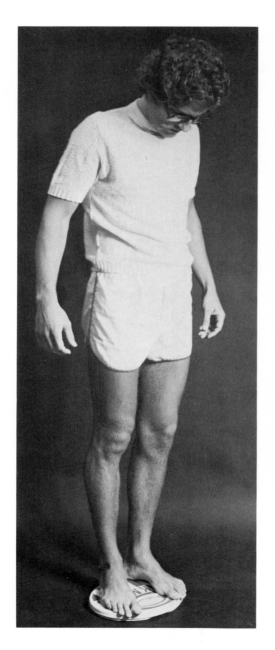

and your mother about 54 kilograms.

A big elephant can have the mass of as much as
6   500 kilograms!

A 10-speed bicycle can have the mass of 13 kilograms.

A medium-sized American car has the mass of about 1 800 kilograms.

The German Shepherd dog down the street has a mass of about 40 kilograms. A little white mouse has a mass of only 25 grams.

If you had a box the size of a cubic meter you could find the mass of even larger things. That box would have the mass of just about one metric ton if you filled it to the top with pure water.

These are the symbols used when measuring the mass of something.

milligram	-	mg
centigram	-	cg
decigram	-	dg
gram	-	g
dekagram	-	dag
hectogram	-	hg
kilogram	-	kg
metric ton	-	t

Remember, the measurements you will use most often for mass are:

GRAM

MILLIGRAM

KILOGRAM

METRIC TON

Now that you know about

the gram

you should meet the rest of
the Metric family.

the metric system is

the liter is

the meter is

the celsius thermometer is

from